A+ books

DINOSAUR FACT DIG

EDMONTOSAURUS

AND OTHER DUCK-BILLED DINOSAURS

THE NEED-TO-KNOW FACTS

BY

REBECCA RISSMAN

Consultant: Mathew J. Wedel, PhD
Associate Professor
Western University of Health Services

raintree
a Capstone company — publishers for children

Raintree is an imprint of Capstone Global Library Limited, a company incorporated in England and Wales having its registered office at 264 Banbury Road, Oxford, OX2 7DY – Registered company number: 6695582

www.raintree.co.uk
myorders@raintree.co.uk

EDITORIAL CREDITS
Michelle Hasselius, editor; Kazuko Collins, designer; Wanda Winch, media researcher; Gene Bentdahl, production specialist

ISBN 978 1 474 7 2826 3
20 19 18 17 16
10 9 8 7 6 5 4 3 2 1

British Library Cataloguing in Publication Data
A full catalogue record for this book is available from the British Library.

ACKNOWLEDGEMENTS
All images by Jon Hughes except: MapArt (maps), Shutterstock: Elena Elisseeva, green gingko leaf, Jiang Hongyan, yellow gingko leaf, Taigi, paper background

We would like to thank Dr Mathew J. Wedel for his invaluable help in the preparation of this book.

Every effort has been made to contact copyright holders of material reproduced in this book. Any omissions will be rectified in subsequent printings if notice is given to the publisher.

All the internet addresses (URLs) given in this book were valid at the time of going to press. However, due to the dynamic nature of the internet, some addresses may have changed, or sites may have changed or ceased to exist since publication. While the author and publisher regret any inconvenience this may cause readers, no responsibility for any such changes can be accepted by either the author or the publisher.

Printed and bound in China.

CONTENTS

Edmontosaurus might have been a dinosaur, but it had a lot in common with today's ducks. Edmontosaurus had a broad, flat bill, similar to a duck's beak. The dinosaur also swam in water.

Edmontosaurus and other duck-billed dinosaurs lived between 85 and 65 million years ago. All dinosaurs in this group had ducklike beaks. Some also had crests on top of their heads. Find out more about Edmontosaurus and other duck-billed dinosaurs, such as Lambeosaurus, Maiasaura and Lophorhothon.

CHARONOSAURUS

PRONOUNCED: shar-OWN-oh-SAWR-us

NAME MEANING: Charon's lizard; named after a Greek mythical figure

TIME PERIOD LIVED: Late Cretaceous Period

LENGTH: 10 metres (32 feet)

WEIGHT: 5 metric tons (5.5 tons)

TYPE OF EATER: herbivore

PHYSICAL FEATURES: sturdy tail; thick legs; large bony crest on its head

CHARONOSAURUS blew through its crest to call to other dinosaurs. It probably sounded like a loud trumpet.

Charonosaurus lived in the forests of what is now China.

N
W ← → E
S

■
where this
dinosaur lived

CHARONOSAURUS walked on four legs. It could also stand up on its back legs to reach tall branches.

Scientists think dinosaurs like **CHARONOSAURUS** had hipbones that looked similar to a bird's hipbones.

CORYTHOSAURUS

PRONOUNCED: KOR-ith-oh-SAWR-us

NAME MEANING: helmet lizard

TIME PERIOD LIVED: Late Cretaceous Period

LENGTH: 8 metres (26 feet)

WEIGHT: 2.7 metric tons (3 tons)

TYPE OF EATER: herbivore

PHYSICAL FEATURES: large teeth; thick legs; large crest on its head

CORYTHOSAURUS probably grazed on ferns and other low-growing plants.

Corythosaurus lived in the forests and swamps of what are now Canada and the United States.

N
W **E**
S

■ where this dinosaur lived

Scientists thought **CORYTHOSAURUS'** crest looked like the helmets worn by ancient Greek soldiers.

Scientists discovered a **CORYTHOSAURUS** fossil that showed what the dinosaur's leathery skin looked like.

EDMONTOSAURUS

PRONOUNCED: ed-MON-toe-SAWR-us

NAME MEANING: royal reptile from Edmonton; named after the Edmonton rock formation, where its fossils were found

TIME PERIOD LIVED: Late Cretaceous Period

LENGTH: 9 metres (30 feet)

WEIGHT: 3.5 metric tons (3.9 tons)

TYPE OF EATER: herbivore

PHYSICAL FEATURES: wide beak; boneless crest on top of its head

EDMONTOSAURUS had up to 2,000 teeth. They locked together to grind up food.

EDMONTOSAURUS ate conifers. It probably also grazed on low plants.

Edmontosaurus lived in the forests and swamps of what are now Canada and the United States.

where this dinosaur lived

N
W E
S

Tyrannosaurus rex was one of **EDMONTOSAURUS'** main predators.

HADROSAURUS

PRONOUNCED: HAD-roh-SAWR-us

NAME MEANING: sturdy lizard

TIME PERIOD LIVED: Late Cretaceous Period

LENGTH: 7 metres (23 feet)

WEIGHT: 2 metric tons (2.2 tons)

TYPE OF EATER: herbivore

PHYSICAL FEATURES: strong legs; short arms; wide beak

HADROSAURUS bones were found in 1858. It was the first dinosaur discovered in North America.

Hadrosaurus lived in the forests and swamps of what is now the United States.

N
W   E
S

where this dinosaur lived

HADROSAURUS was the first dinosaur to have its skeleton put on display.

HADROSAURUS lived in big herds, similar to other dinosaurs in this group.

KRITOSAURUS

PRONOUNCED: KRIT-oh-SAWR-us

NAME MEANING: separated lizard

TIME PERIOD LIVED: Late Cretaceous Period

LENGTH: 8 metres (26 feet)

WEIGHT: 3 metric tons (3.3 tons)

TYPE OF EATER: herbivore

PHYSICAL FEATURES: long legs and tail; short arms; small crest

KRITOSAURUS got its name because its cheekbones did not fit together well when it was first discovered.

Kritosaurus lived in the forests and swamps of what is now the southern United States.

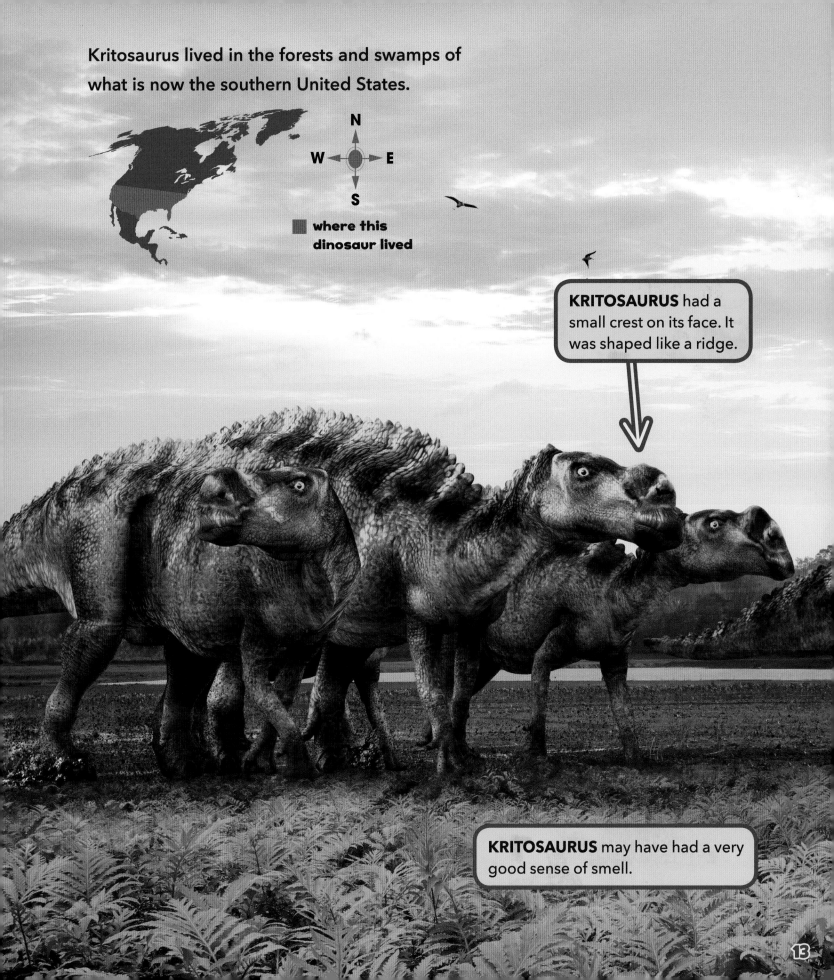

N
W   E
S

■ where this dinosaur lived

KRITOSAURUS had a small crest on its face. It was shaped like a ridge.

KRITOSAURUS may have had a very good sense of smell.

LAMBEOSAURUS

PRONOUNCED: lam-BEE-oh-SAWR-us

NAME MEANING: Lambe's lizard; named after Lawrence Lambe, a famous paleontologist

TIME PERIOD LIVED: Late Cretaceous Period

LENGTH: 9 metres (29 feet)

WEIGHT: 2.4 metric tons (2.6 tons)

TYPE OF EATER: herbivore

PHYSICAL FEATURES: strong beak; large mitten-shaped crest on its head

LAMBEOSAURUS had a strong beak with many teeth to eat tough plants.

LAMBEOSAURUS could probably hear very well.

Lambeosaurus lived in the forests and swamps of what are now Canada, Mexico and the United States.

N
W E
S

where this dinosaur lived

Scientists have had many ideas about how **LAMBEOSAURUS** used its crest. One was that the dinosaur used it as a snorkel to swim underwater.

LOPHORHOTHON

PRONOUNCED: LOF-or-HOH-thon

NAME MEANING: crested nose

TIME PERIOD LIVED: Late Cretaceous Period

LENGTH: 4.5 metres (15 feet)

WEIGHT: 1.8 metric tons (2 tons)

TYPE OF EATER: herbivore

PHYSICAL FEATURES: short arms; strong legs; small crest over its eyes

LOPHORHOTHON may have chewed tough plants for a long time before swallowing, like cows do today.

Lophorhothon lived in the forests of what is now the United States.

N
W E
S

where this dinosaur lived

LOPHORHOTHON had a very thick, strong tail.

The first **LOPHORHOTHON** fossils were discovered in Alabama, USA in 1940.

MAIASAURA

PRONOUNCED: MY-a-SAWR-uh

NAME MEANING: good mother lizard

TIME PERIOD LIVED: Late Cretaceous Period

LENGTH: 7 metres (23 feet)

WEIGHT: 2.5 metric tons (2.8 tons)

TYPE OF EATER: herbivore

PHYSICAL FEATURES: tail used for balance; narrow beak; small crests over its eyes

Scientists have discovered **MAIASAURA** nests. They have found fossils of unhatched eggs, babies and adults inside the nests.

Maiasaura lived in the forests of what is now the United States.

It took about seven or eight years for **MAIASAURA** to reach full size.

N
W   E
S

where this dinosaur lived

Fossils show that **MAIASAURA** babies could not walk right away. They needed to be cared for by adults.

OLOROTITAN

PRONOUNCED: oh-LAW-roh-TYE-tan

NAME MEANING: giant swan

TIME PERIOD LIVED: Late Cretaceous Period

LENGTH: 8 metres (26 feet)

WEIGHT: 3.1 metric tons (3.4 tons)

TYPE OF EATER: herbivore

PHYSICAL FEATURES: stiff tail; long neck; fan-shaped crest on its head

OLOROTITAN probably used its long neck to bite leaves from tall trees.

where this dinosaur lived

N
W E
S

Olorotitan lived in the forests of what is now Russia.

OLOROTITAN could have used its crest to scare away other dinosaurs, similar to what frilled lizards do today.

Another theory is dinosaurs like **OLOROTITAN** may have used their crests to identify one another.

PARASAUROLOPHUS

PRONOUNCED: PAR-uh-SAWR-oh-LOH-fus

NAME MEANING: like Saurolophus; Saurolophus was another duck-billed dinosaur with a smaller crest

TIME PERIOD LIVED: Late Cretaceous Period

LENGTH: 7.5 metres (25 feet)

WEIGHT: 2.6 metric tons (2.9 tons)

TYPE OF EATER: herbivore

PHYSICAL FEATURES: beak; long crest on its head; strong legs

PARASAUROLOPHUS is one of the most famous duck-billed dinosaurs because of its unique crest.

Parasaurolophus lived in the forests of what is now the United States and Canada.

N
W — E
S

where this dinosaur lived

PARASAUROLOPHUS was discovered in 1922 by paleontologist William Parks. The dinosaur Parksosaurus was named in honour of Parks.

At first scientists thought that **PARASAUROLOPHUS** used its crest to fight other dinosaurs. Today few scientists think this theory is true.

SAUROLOPHUS

PRONOUNCED: SAWR-oh-LOH-fus

NAME MEANING: ridged lizard

TIME PERIOD LIVED: Late Cretaceous Period

LENGTH: 8.2 metres (27 feet)

WEIGHT: 3 metric tons (3.3 tons)

TYPE OF EATER: herbivore

PHYSICAL FEATURES: strong legs; thick tail; spike-shaped crest on its head

SAUROLOPHUS could run and walk on its back legs. This may have helped the dinosaur to escape from predators.

Saurolophus lived in the forests and swamps of what are now Canada and Mongolia.

N
W ← E
S

where this dinosaur lived

Paleontologist Barnum Brown named **SAUROLOPHUS**. Brown was a famous fossil hunter who discovered the first Tyrannosaurus rex.

SAUROLOPHUS may have had a brightly coloured crest. This could have helped it stand out to other dinosaurs.

SHANTUNGOSAURUS

PRONOUNCED: SHAN-tung-oh-SAWR-us

NAME MEANING: Shandong lizard; fossils were first discovered in the Shandong, China

TIME PERIOD LIVED: Late Cretaceous Period

LENGTH: 15 metres (50 feet)

WEIGHT: 13 metric tons (14.3 tons)

TYPE OF EATER: herbivore

PHYSICAL FEATURES: wide beak; thick legs; strong arms

SHANTUNGOSAURUS had more than 1,000 teeth.

Shantungosaurus lived in what is now China.

N
W E
S

where this
dinosaur lived

An adult **SHANTUNGOSAURUS**
was longer than a school bus.

SHANTUNGOSAURUS' thighbone
was more than 1.8 metres (6 feet) long.

TSINTAOSAURUS

PRONOUNCED: SIN-tow-SAWR-us

NAME MEANING: Tsingtao lizard; fossils were first discovered in Tsingtao, China

TIME PERIOD LIVED: Late Cretaceous Period

LENGTH: 8.2 metres (27 feet)

WEIGHT: 2.5 metric tons (2.8 tons)

TYPE OF EATER: herbivore

PHYSICAL FEATURES: strong legs; thick tail; beak; fan-shaped crest on top of its head

TSINTAOSAURUS grew new teeth after its old teeth wore down.

Tsintaosaurus lived in what is now China.

N
W E
S

■ where this
dinosaur lived

TSINTAOSAURUS had many
flat teeth in order to chew
through tough plants.

For a long time, scientists thought
TSINTAOSAURUS' crest looked like a unicorn's
horn. Newly discovered fossils show that its crest
was shaped like a fan, similar to the crests of
Corythosaurus and Olorotitan.

GLOSSARY

ANCIENT from a long time ago

BEAK hard part of a bird's mouth; some dinosaurs had beaks

CONIFER tree with cones and narrow leaves called needles

CREST flat plate of bone

CRETACEOUS PERIOD third period of the Mesozoic Era; the Cretaceous Period was from 145 to 65 million years ago

FERN plant with long, thin leaves called fronds

FOSSIL remains of an animal or plant from millions of years ago that have turned to rock

FRILLED LIZARD large lizard with a broad frill on each side of its neck; frilled lizards live in Australia

GRAZE eat grass and other plants growing in fields

HERBIVORE animal that eats only plants

HERD large group of animals that lives or travels together

IDENTIFY tell what something is or who someone is

PALEONTOLOGIST scientist who studies fossils

PREDATOR animal that hunts other animals for food

PRONOUNCE say a word in a certain way

SNORKEL tube used to breathe through when swimming underwater

THEORY idea that explains something that is unknown

TRUMPET musical instrument with a long, looped tube that ends in a funnel shape, with three valves used to change the tones

COMPREHENSION QUESTIONS

1. Tyrannosaurus rex was one of Edmontosaurus' main predators. What is a predator?

2. What was the name of the first dinosaur discovered in North America?

3. Describe two ways Olorotitan could have used its crest.

READ MORE

Dinosaurs! (Knowledge Encyclopedia), DK (DK Children, 2014)

Dinosaurs in our Streets, David West (Franklin Watts, 2015)

Meet Edmontosaurus (The Age of Dinosaurs), Dean Miller and Sheryn Knight (Cavendish Square Publishing, 2014)

WEBSITES

www.nhm.ac.uk/discover/dino-directory/index.html
At this Natural History Museum website you can learn more about dinosaurs through sorting them by name, country and even body shape!

www.show.me.uk/section/dinosaurs
This website has loads of fun things to do and see, including a dinosaur mask you can download and print, videos, games and Top Ten lists.

INDEX